The Beginner's Bible™ Adventure Series
Super Coloring & Activity Book

Story Time with
Jesus
Parables

THE BEGINNERS BIBLE™

LANDOLL'S®

® LANDOLL, INC.
ASHLAND, OHIO 44805

This is Mary and Joseph. They loved each other very much.

One day an angel named Gabriel told Mary she would have God's Son.

Which angel is different?

Mary wondered how this could happen. Gabriel told her that nothing was impossible with God. Mary believed Gabriel.

Mary and Joseph traveled to the city of Bethlehem. There was no room for Mary and Joseph at the inn.

The innkeeper let Mary and Joseph stay in his stable.

Just as the angel Gabriel had promised, a baby was born. He was God's Son. And Mary and Joseph named him Jesus.

An angel appeared to the shepherds while they watched their sheep.
The angel said, "God's Son was born in Bethlehem. Go see him."

Count the angels and write the total here: ____

ANSWER: 17

Then many angels appeared to the shepherds. They sang and praised God saying, "Glory to God and peace on earth."

The shepherds traveled to Bethlehem to find God's Son.

Help the shepherds find baby Jesus.

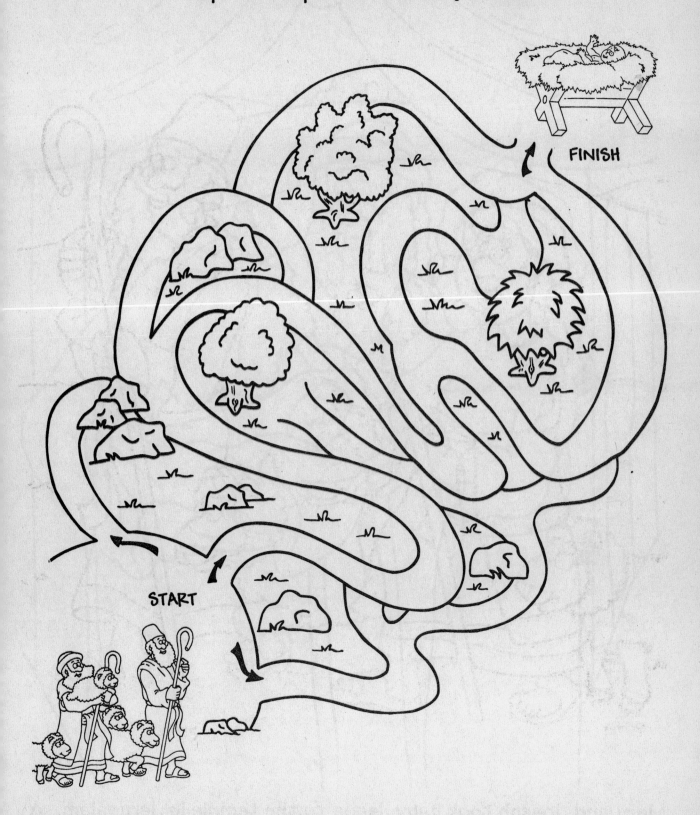

FINISH

START

The shepherds found baby Jesus in the stable.

Mary and Joseph took baby Jesus to the temple in Jerusalem. A priest named Simeon praised baby Jesus and sang a song.

Three wise men followed a bright star in the heavens. They knew the star would lead them to God's Son.

Unscramble the words about baby Jesus.

YAMR _____

MRYRH _____

WSEI NEM _____

DLOG _____

TFSGI _____

BYBA _____

RTAS _____

BELSTA _____

EHJOPS _____

KNIFESECNNAR _____

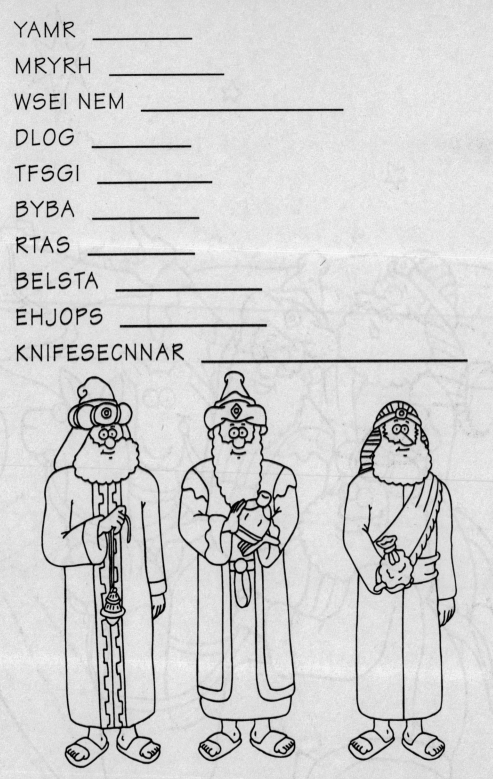

ANSWERS: MARY, MYRRH, WISE MEN, GOLD, GIFTS, BABY, STAR, STABLE, JOSEPH, FRANKINCENSE

The wise men brought gifts of gold, frankincense and myrrh for the newborn king.

Connect the dots to make Joseph's tools.

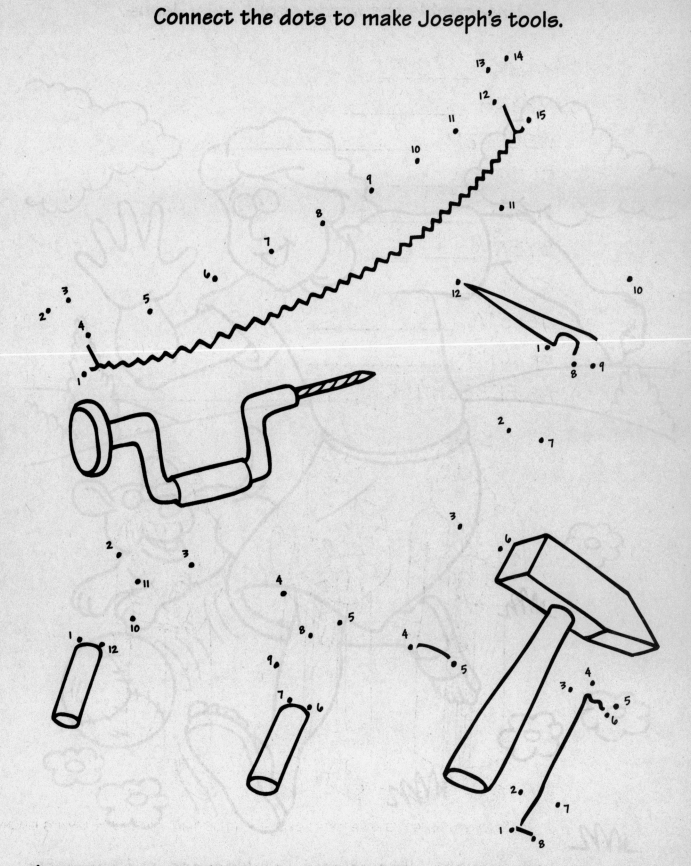

Jesus grew up in the town of Nazareth. He learned how to be a carpenter from Joseph.

Jesus was like other children. He loved to run and play!

Mary and Joseph took Jesus to the temple in Jerusalem. Many of their friends went with them.

Later, Mary and Joseph could not find Jesus. They asked everyone, but no one knew where he was.

Mary and Joseph hurried back to the temple. There they found
Jesus talking to the priests about God.

There once was a man named John The Baptist. He lived in the
desert and ate locusts and wild honey.

Many people thought John The Baptist was Jesus, but John was chosen by God to tell people about Jesus.

One day Jesus came to John and was baptized. This made John very happy.

As soon as Jesus came out of the water, the spirit of God came down to him in the form of a dove.

Jesus prayed to God. He had very important work to do, and he needed some special helpers.

Jesus saw Peter, Andrew, James and John fishing. He waved to them and said, "Come and follow me."

Jesus saw a man named Matthew counting money. Matthew quit his job and followed Jesus, too.

Jesus chose 7 other men to be his helpers. They told people about God.

At a wedding, the servers ran out of wine. Jesus turned the water into wine.

Jesus used stories called parables to teach people about God.
One day, Jesus told a story about forgiving others.

Help the younger son find his way to the city.

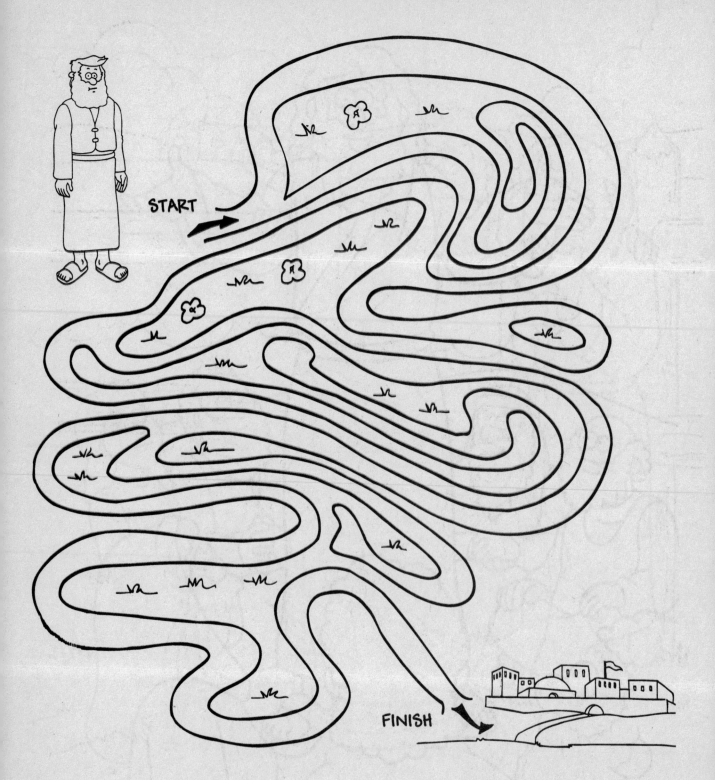

START

FINISH

Once there was a man with two sons. The younger son asked his father for money. He wanted the money so he could travel.

The father loved his son very much, so he gave him the money.
The younger son packed his things and set off to see the world.

When the younger son arrived in the city he bought the most expensive clothes he could find.

But he soon ran out of money. He did not even have enough money to buy a piece of bread.

Use the code to learn something about the prodigal son.

A	B	C	D	E	F	G	H	I	J	K	L	M
26	25	24	23	22	21	20	19	18	17	16	15	14

N	O	P	Q	R	S	T	U	V	W	X	Y	Z
13	12	11	10	9	8	7	6	5	4	3	2	1

___ ___ ___   ___ ___ ___ ___ ___ ___ ___ ___
7 19 22   11 9 12 23 18 20 26 15

___ ___ ___   ___ ___ ___ ___   ___ ___ ___ ___
8 12 13   15 22 21 7   19 12 14 22

___ ___ ___
26 13 23

___ ___ ___ ___ ___
8 11 22 13 7

___ ___ ___   ___ ___ ___
26 15 15   19 18 8

___ ___ ___ ___ ___ .
14 12 13 22 2

The younger son decided to return home and ask his father if he could work for him.

When the father saw his son, he ran to meet him. The son said, "Father, I was wrong to leave you. Please forgive me and let me work for you."

Unscramble the words about the prodigal son.

ROPDGILA NOS _____ _____

HATREF _____

MOHE _____

YMENO _____

SGIP _____

EVOL _____

GRFIVOE _____

CTHLOSE _____

DOFO _____

TYRAP _____

The father was happy to see his son. He kissed him and said, "We will have a party to celebrate your return home."

The older son was told that his younger brother had come home. The older son was angry. He refused to go inside to see his brother.

The father said, "You have been safe here with me. But your brother who I thought was lost, is alive. We must forgive him and celebrate."

Jesus traveled from city to city telling about God's love. He cared about people who did not know God. This confused some of the men at the temple.

One day Jesus heard them say, "Why does he spend time with people who do not know God?"

Which sheep is different?

ANSWER: 5

Jesus told them the story of the lost sheep to help them understand.

Help the shepherd find his lost sheep.

Once there was a shepherd who spent every day watching over his sheep.
He had 100 sheep to watch over.

Find the hidden words that tell about the good shepherd.

```
L  I  N  S  H  E  P  H  E  R  D
O  L  T  H  R  O  T  L  N  O  O
V  G  O  E  G  S  T  A  I  R
E  E  A  E  T  T  R  R  C  R  F
G  O  D  P  A  S  T  U  R  E  O
P  S  R  L  A  C  A  R  E  K  O
G  S  W  O  O  L  K  E  R  A  D
R  O  K  S  F  R  I  E  N  D  S
T  W  A  T  E  R  G  R  A  S  S
```

FIND THESE WORDS

LOVE
GOD
SHEPHERD
LOST
SHEEP
WOOL
WATER
GRASS
FRIENDS
PASTURE
FOOD
CARE

Each morning, the shepherd led his sheep to the pasture. There they had grass to eat and plenty of water to drink.

The shepherd counted his sheep as he put them back in the pen. One evening, he counted only 99 sheep. One was lost!

The shepherd looked everywhere for the one lost sheep.

Finally he found the sheep. He placed it on his shoulders and carried it home.

Help the people find their way to the good shepherd.

The shepherd was happy! He called his friends and told them his good news.

Unscramble the words about the good shepherd.

EPESH _____

TRPASUE _____

HDSERPHE _____

LOOW _____

VOLE _____

TSOL _____

FODO _____

NIRDK _____

SASRG _____

SDIRFNE _____

Jesus wanted the men from the temple to know that God cares for all people. Even those who are lost and have not found God.